# Heartfelt Words

# Heartfelt Words

Leroy Vincent

# CONTENTS

First Printing, 2024

# 1

# Introduction

Heartfelt Words is not just an ordinary quote book. It is a meticulously compiled work covering a wide range of relationship quotes for couples – for those in love, those in relationships, or bringing up families. These quotes are designed to give you inspiration and guidance towards building a strong and healthy relationship. Love is personal and relationships are unique, so the look of your love life will be very different to everybody else's. They are designed to support you, to guide you, to encourage you, and to inspire you to reach the best of your relationship, no matter how good it is!

This book is filled with pretty words for people who are falling in love and those who are already in love. Falling in love is the most beautiful sensation in a human being's life. One does not know what happened when you fall in love as it's sudden and appears to lead you in a quest of love and adaptation with your lover. This book is filled with some of the most inspirational words for those who are experiencing issues in their relationship. More than three hundred thoughtful quotes have been included in this book to help them think about their love and consider what scale of action is needed to solve issues. No couple comes across and meets without future prediction in their part of the loving world. Every couple fights, argues but what turns into positive and how to stop troubles with loch some heartfelt words from 'same heart' is creating level of eight difference in every person to give a bit of emotional support.

## Purpose of the Book

Hello there. If you are reading this, you are likely looking to the future of your love. I am hoping for a similar future, since I have decided that my search for knowledge and personal satisfaction is not quite complete. You see, as a poet, I am always trying to convey the emotions between a person and God. And, as I once said, a marriage or loving partnership between two people is supposed to be a miniature version of the union we share with God.

Correct me if I am wrong, but people and couples are looking for ways to better balance their time between each other and a higher power such as God. My hope is to address the issues regarding the central idea of the impossible relationship by using a shrine to love. My pen name, 'Nausicaa', comes from Greek mythology. 'Nausicaa' is known as the "face that launched 100 ships". She is the story about the woman who washes ashore a nobleman and cares for him without asking for anything in return. This is just an overview of my story, but what does the story of "SEA" have to do with love quotes? Honestly, very little. However, the sentiment behind it is what I am aiming to convey. In other words, the primary objective of this book is to inspire love between two people in a non-religious way, and specifically the timeless love between two individuals who will also grow to be 'of one flesh and spirit' over time.

## Benefits of Using Love Quotes in Relationships

One of the sweetest ways to express your love for someone is with the help of the words of others. Integrating love quotes into your correspondence with your special someone is a breath of fresh air. There is an abundance of admiration, love, and passion in the universe. There is also bountiful knowledge, tradition, and an abundance of love at any era and within all cultures. People have been in love as long as there have been people. Long before our time, people were struck on the arse by Cupid's arrow. And, as long as there have been hearts aflutter with romance, love quotes have come to pass. There's an abundance of love quotes to suit every imaginable circumstance because every feel-good love story, poem, and painting owe it to love itself. Love is not only a subject worth exploring and extolling; it is the entity that inspires life itself.

So there are not only lots of quotes about love but also love affirmations, and love quotes are the heart and soul of love affirmations. Our love relationships can be transformed by love quotes. Some quotations about appreciating love and nurturing emotions can have a profound effect on us, challenging us to have faith and giving us the courage to make our feelings known. Furthermore, most quotes about love come from display of emotions that are not only easier to articulate than emotions. Nonetheless, many quotations regarding love are created by guys. While we might wish that there were more love affirmations on behalf of women, our hearts hold true with the love affirmations we have. Some of the best love quotes and affirmations are those which illustrate the beauty and sensitivity of love, which is not only taken but which we submit to others in anticipation and faith of returning our love. A tough go of things is what many of us have put our hearts and perceptive relationships through. Every so often, we only require a little help. Out of their extensive knowledge and feelings, friendship quotations, quotes and sayings with love in them.

2

# Chapter 1: Building a Strong Foundation

There are a few fundamental aspects which can help us build a dedication. Though it may not seem like it at times, our relationship has a mission, a purpose that was established at the very beginning. Even if we can't put those pragmatic words up front yet, we know our partnership should be built on a lasting promise. This idea of a dedication allows time for necessary growth until we can comfortably let our hearts announce the commitment that every relationship should express. It goes beyond saying it, beyond just feeling it to a point where it is untouchable and overpowering as part of our shared reality. There are many things that we must carefully examine in wise rededication to one another.

Starting with the basics, the first step in building a mission for our relationship is making a solid commitment. Let us begin on a road to developing our own covenant. Achieving fame for our commitment is not our primary goal. We want to lead ourselves to true investment in us. Rededicating ourselves to our shared mission each day begins in places such as your reading of this guide. Our commitment becomes stronger through counseling and common interest. Working and playing together: As we become stronger, our positive treatment of one another also becomes a part of that fabric. Making true our shared goals: Yet another way to improve dedication is by acting as a team. Every day, working together towards our goals is a way to build mission fulfillment.

## Understanding the Power of Words

Feeling Love: Can Words Really Make That Big an Impact?

Few things can impact our hearts as quickly and deeply as words—just reading or hearing our special someone's sweet nothings to us can fill us with warmth and happiness. This phenomenon seems to be especially present in the world of love and relationships. Complimenting our significant others or talking to them about how beautiful or talented or incredible they are not only makes them feel good, but can keep emotional and verbal intimacy bursting at the seams.

We all have our love languages, things or behaviors that we love being done to and around us to make us feel connected to our partners. But so many of us, regardless of our unique combinations of our love languages, also find extreme value in hearing the sweet nothings our partners want to make sure we hear. When we humans fall head over heels for someone—and the feeling's mutual—the drive to not just indulge in, but to make these precious words commonplace is deeply encoded in our hearts. It seems to make bonding and forging a relationship of depth and security easier. In the same stroke, when both partners' needs for hearing heartwarming declarations are linked by a shared power of expression, there is an extra cohesiveness to appreciate. A solid relationship bolstered by sweet, soppy words around every corner makes for a heart, mind, and spirit-melting union. So, want to keep that loving glow walking and talking in your chests? Flamboyantly use all of the gushy, affectionate, loving words you can in your interactions with one another.

## Communication and Connection

One of the essential aspects of a relationship is how well it begins. A relationship should build gradually from a foundation of mutual attraction and respect. Your needs and wants should not be laid bare at your first meeting. Gradually getting to know each other is also a good test of the strength of your desires and commitments to the relationship. When two people meet, they usually put their best foot forward. The question you have to ask yourself is: Has your partner kept up the same level of ideals and standards they showed you in the early part of your relationship?

Towards the beginning of a new relationship, love can be turned slightly blind. I stress "slightly" because many attributes can be faked. If you are honest with yourself asking this question, you may get reflect and ask, "Have you also stuck to the values and ideas your partner expected from you early in the relationship?"

During this building phase of the relationship, don't tell your partner all your worries and problems. In fact, telling your mate all your personal issues are likely to turn them away. They want to date someone who is more secure. Stick to things of general interest; don't get too heavy.

When to Test Your Relationship

This chapter also discusses some important times when many relationships fall apart due to classic errors. I often hear women say "Why did he change...?" when quite often, he didn't change. Rather, the person who changed was you. You suddenly decided to make an effort to not be the real you in the hope of strengthening your relationship. Women seek advice at this point in desperation at seeing their man withdraw yet, in the new relationship, they were giving out enticements such as sex, only for the man to meter out attention of any sort including touching. In other words, he established she wanted him so made her go wide in her manner, yet after he felt he had her all to himself, retreated to the degree he wanted.

It is a good idea to review these points, make a mental note and when personal experiences crop up, make a second mental note, comparing the new experience with the views expressed in this chapter. Talk over any disagreements with your partner, see if they also agree with the contents of this book to help speed your new relationship towards a successful relationship. Be honest with each other.

3

# Chapter 2: Nurturing Love and Affection

Introduction This chapter provides practical advice on making love happen. It underscores the importance of practical expressions and displays of love, calls for a bit more love to come from the heart, notes the need to look for the good in your beloved instead of brooding over his/her shortcomings, and invites the reader to acknowledge and share in his or her beloved's hopes and dreams. In short, only attempted acts of love make real love grow. For love is the result of practiced deeds, not an abstract principle to be lived by default.

The Necessity of Love Practical love ornaments, actual displays of love are the basis of every successful relationship. It is the demonstration of love rather than its utterance that promotes a lasting and deeper love. Love permeates even the simplest acts: a smile, a word, a touch always have a much deeper intended purpose. Such acts inspire love more than hearing it over and over. In the attempt to convey love, a look becomes a smile of understanding and a kind word, the comfort of support. The stronger the bond, the greater the need for such deeds. A smile is not yet love, but it paves the way for it. And whenever a look, a word, or a touch perceives the affection of the other person, this insight is uplifting. Provided that conveyed love is heartfelt.

Nurturing Partners Spirit Love bears all things and has the gift to offer the grace of being refined through the roughness of life. No one is perfect. We all have our strengths and weaknesses, and they are part of what makes us who we are. Whenever fault is found, always do so with kindness and without hurting feelings. Recognize opportunities and possibilities and show an interest in them. Encourage your partner in his or her choices, dreams, and hopes and lend an attentive ear. When you do that, love shows itself, and not only does the power of love embrace the soul, but also the deepest core of being human. That power deepens the bond.

## Expressing Gratitude and Appreciation

In relationships, it's always the little things that count. Emotions are the fuel of any love story. This is why, rather than giving grandiose and excessive presents, we recommend speaking from the heart. Send upbeat love quotes to your friends and family. Talk to your soul mate about romantic themes. Surprise your idol with a romantic quote in an unexpected location. The terminology of love is limitless. Friends or family, this delicate and intimate word is bound to resonate with your mate. Have a look at our assortment of uplifting quotes to spread warmth and sentiment.

One of the most essential aspects of a relationship is acknowledging and appreciating the many gems. Little acts of romance will effectively communicate your esteem and admiration for your companion. These three categories will leave an individual feeling fuzzy and deeply loved. Begin with thanks for the tiny things. Your friend likes mealtimes and often eats with you to unwind. Tell him how important this appeal to share togetherness while conversing about the day's activities. Often, it's important to say how valuable this practice of showing the wrath that you already have its perfect aspect with particular gratitude.

### Acts of Kindness and Thoughtfulness

Of course, expressions of love are not limited to individual, distinct moments. They are an ongoing, changing series of words and physical acts, of kind things done, of time spent in pleasant togetherness. They are nourished by simple, everyday actions: a well-prepared dinner, an unexpected cleaning of the house, a cup of morning coffee prepared with loving attention, anything, small or large, showing that we are getting to know what the beloved might appreciate and extending ourselves to offer it to them. In this view, it is not the grandest funeral or the most passionate declaration of love that keeps a couple together, but the series of small, loving acts that forge their most immediate connection, day in, day out. Whomever we love, that person is a burly, heavy kit, full of hopes and feelings and stuff that makes her ache and laugh, and we are a kit equally vexing. Love means rendering each other's kits more habitable because it acknowledges the difference made by the other human wobbling within.

Love is forever on the quest to understand the beloved more deeply and to serve her in ways that her soul is crying out for. And, of course, in receiving a kind and thoughtful act from the beloved, the lover can see and gently celebrate in himself that part of him that called out for the consolation, the understanding, or the warm touch. The lover who runs to offer his beloved's heart a warm embrace in the face of loss knows, in a deep and spiritual way, that this is the very thing he is bursting for, too. He hurries, smiling, because he knows himself. Therefore, he can recognize it in the face of others, too.

4

# Chapter 3: Overcoming Challenges Together

This chapter is about how it's necessary for us to challenge in life for the couple to be strong. When there are challenges, the couple needs to work hard together to stay together as one: for two people to become one entity. By overcoming these challenges, the bond between the two people becomes stronger, and marriage becomes valuable. However, if one of the couple loses the motivation to overcome the challenges and withdraws, the relationship will be weakened. It's not about how the two of them will be the ones who are happier, but how they can be the happiest in the process of uniting the two! I wanted to show how essential it is for two people to contribute and achieve the bond.

Throughout life, there will be many difficulties and causes of anxiety. A person can feel joy or hope and, as a result, can find good things from bad experiences. Generally, the outcome of things or incidents depends on proper management and how you respond to fear. Relationships between values and happiness are positive; the more value a person has to his or her happiness, the happier they are. Couples who engage in things that they consider highly beneficial are less likely to split up. In other words, couples are more fortunate and comfortable than couples who are not as committed as they are because they place great significance on the good of couple relationships and the benefits of communion. For this reason, couples who overcome difficult times in their relationship will become closer as time goes on.

### Conflict Resolution and Compromise

Conflict resolution is one of the most essential pillars of any healthy, happy love relationship. Because no two people are ever going to agree on absolutely everything all the time, the ability to engage in effective communication, find mutually acceptable solutions, and make healthy compromises is imperative to establishing a foundation of mutual respect and collaboration that can help couples work through their differences. Here are the facts about how to communicate and find a healthy, acceptable compromise with your partner.

Resolve everything in a healthy and resolving manner. While it is likely that not all arguments can be resolved before bedtime, making a pact with your loved one to address every conflict with love and compassion will help to ensure that bad feelings don't linger and breed into something worse. Make a point not to let little things fester and grow into big, angry arguments by utilizing quick and honest communication to establish understanding between both of you. Talk about things before they become an issue. Make a concerted effort not to go to bed on a fight – studies have shown that people are less able to make healthy compromises when they're tired and stressed, and tend to rely on less healthy, more aggressive response patterns. That's one of the last things you want when you're trying to work through a negotiation. If you're working to get something important settled between the two of you, give it the proper focus and attention it requires, especially when the stakes are high. While it's good to take quiet time and to clear your head in order to gather your thoughts, it can be equally helpful to schedule a time to address bigger concerns, especially if you'd like to be sure to make the most of the limited amount of time you have together.

## Supporting Each Other Through Difficult Times

One of the most rewarding things about love is how it provides a sturdy foundation for supporting one another. In the midst of verbiage about how love conquers all, we sometimes forget that it's the support of a loving relationship that bolsters us after a tough day at school or work, takes the sting out of the hard times, and angles us straight toward the next sunny field of hope. Great partners know that it's important to make the time and make the effort to actively support each other, especially when faced with hard times. Here are some tips for how you and your honey can coach each other through the tough stuff and avoid getting lost along the way.

• 7. Remember to stand by your partner in tough times: It should go without saying, but everyone, and everyone's parents and grandparents, "likes to be around people positive to them in times of success, but need a person with whom [they] can share their sorrow is as important as is the sharing of their happiness at their success." • 8. Don't tell your partner to snap out of it or toughen up: Irrationally furious with your project group members? Crying over spilt milk? Living under a constant evil clown infestation? Of course your partner isn't upset about those (both because they're irrational and because he doesn't share your evil clown phobia), but let him have his pity party for the moment—as long as it's a matter of minutes or hours, not days. If there's something he can do to fix the situation, step in with helpful suggestions. • 9. Simply lend a shoulder and offer some injectable anesthetic advice: Just lend a good, caring shoulder related to 7. At some point. Offer "soft words," saying something like, "I know this hurts you."

5

# Chapter 4: Celebrating Love and Milestones

Paragraph: Celebrating love should be important in a person's life. When we celebrate love, we celebrate the joining of two people who have committed their lives to each other. How deeply we feel love when we celebrate our love! How much greater we feel! The memories of these days can hold a special charm.

Paragraph: Discovering how much a person is loved by the one chosen to marry is glorious indeed! So, what glorious days are celebrated and how do they make one feel? Below are the days when love and life's celebrations intertwine. Each of these days marks a milestone in a marriage and is an anniversary of love. These are the days that are not meant to be overlooked; instead, they are to be celebrated to the fullest. Acknowledge love with each of the following days. They are just as important as the day love was married.

- The Day Love Was Married - The Month Love Was Married - The Week Love Was Married - The Day Love Proposed

It is wonderful to create your own lifelong traditions surrounding the days mentioned above. It could be such a wonderful way to honor and celebrate love by having a family dinner on the day love was married and serve your wedding meal. Decorating can be scaled down; you can set a nice table with candles, play soft music, and wear something special. Use the formal dishes and lace tablecloth. Once dinner is done, watch your wedding video or look at old photo albums and reminisce. It is also fun to exchange small gifts.

## Creating Meaningful Rituals and Traditions

"Ritual can ease pain, comfort the spirit, and convey love and connection, such as the quiet comfort of greeting one's partner with a hug and kiss daily as soon as you open the door," says Rabbi Sassi-Keshet. "Traditions, which carry all the weight of historical continuity and can draw people from different generations together in a kind of continuous dance, can be one of the glues that hold a couple together." It's natural to want to establish these customs with a partner.

These customs can be anything that brings you two closer together that you both find meaningful. You can take inspiration from religious and cultural customs or borrow from things you grew up with (one of your traditions may already be having Sunday dinner with the family). And customs aren't only for couples who've been married for decades. They can offer familiarity and a sense of continuity (as in, we do this because we always have) even within new or beginning relationships. "One advantage of creating meaningful rituals for your marriage when you are still in a honeymoon phase is that you grow from the experiences simultaneously," says Sassi-Keshet. "Ritual itself can become a teaching tool as you reflect on whatever you have chosen for your ritual and seen how each of you has changed over time."

## Honoring Special Occasions

It is important - some will say even imperative - to be sure to give credit, and sometimes to give special acknowledgment when it comes to planning for and creating the gifting of special occasions with specialty and recognition. These moments needed to be transformed - uplifted to feel reminded of the plethora of love available to not only surround us but flow through and exist within us, as well. There are a few strategies to strengthen your love and let your partner know they are worthy of a little extra effort.

Chalk it up to the power of making someone feel extraordinary. When we sense that we are being seen, we are not only accessible as a whole human with a variety of needs, but more accessible for the things that need to flow through us, as well. In the end, it all results in simpler interactions, easier decision-making, and closer bonds with those you care about. Most dating, love, and test drives in your love realm are found within the journey - awake to all that is around you, and pushed away from what was in favor of the experience that fills you. For most of us, life is a whole lot more about the everyday, rather than the "wow!", but still needs to intertwine within them carefully if we are to make them the most interesting, rich, and full moments that good relationships tend to turn out to be.

6

# Chapter 5: Sustaining Love for the Long Haul

If it's realistic to say nearly 50% of relationships end in breakups, and we also know that it's normal for so-called "honeymoon love" to fade, we can safely attest to bad habits and attitudes ruining the best relationships. This chapter is dedicated to what is required to create lasting love and sustained passion over time. The key is to nurture and care for your attachment to each other through continued positive interactions to answer the needs and trust investment that is required to sustain a relationship over the long haul.

Focusing on the Mate's Needs • One of the biggest myths of lasting love is the belief that it just happens, or that some are just lucky enough to have mates who fulfill their needs while they do not have to sacrifice their own. The truth is that romantic expectations dampen passion and desire, leading to feelings of disappointment, inadequacy, and rejection.

Nurturing Love for the Long Haul • In order to go the extra mile of investment in efforts to keep love alive, internal positive motivations and attitudes are required. Hoping to get an equal return on investment over time can inspire feelings of discontent and resentment. Long-term love requires a high level of interpersonal skills and practices beyond romantic love and attraction, such as negotiating needs, wishes, and interpersonal differences. Passion is a journey against societal influences.

### Renewing and Reaffirming Commitment

One of the most valuable ways love quotes can strengthen your bond is by renewing and reaffirming commitment. Long-term commitment requires a series of smaller commitments over time, and it can be easy to forget or lose sight of these when life gets busy or love gets complicated. The quotes above provide inspiration for rekindling and reinforcing your dedication to one another, but they only work if you let them. It can be tempting to brush off such sentimentality as nothing but empty words, but words are powerful. If you rephrase or reflect upon these quotes in terms of your own experiences, you are likely to feel a spark.

In essence, even just reading these loving sentiments can assist you in finding a way to believe in them in terms of yourself and your life. Plus, as with all things, the more you practice and the more you believe, the stronger the sentiment grows. You can make your love life more fulfilling by reflecting on these inspirational quotes and using them as talking points and discussion starters. Discuss metaphors in the quotes you read or talk about ways love looks different to different people. If you are lost for words or looking to delight your partner with well-thought-out romantic gestures, consider discussing these quotes and what inspires you about them.

### Growing Together as Individuals and as a Couple

Wilferd Peterson has an inspirational quote about love: "The art of a happy marriage is in the ability to be two at the same time." Couples do not lose their individuality in a loving relationship; instead, a couple is a partnership of two unique individuals. Take a look at the motivational words of wisdom that have been gathered in this section. These quotes contain advice on everything from taking time to communicate to maintaining balance within a relationship.

"Love possesses not nor will it be possessed, for love is sufficient unto love. Love has no other desire but to fulfill itself... But if you love and must needs have desires, let these be your desires: To melt and be like a running brook that sings its melody to the night. To know the pain of too much tenderness. To be wounded by your own understanding of love; And to bleed willingly and joyfully." - Kahlil Gibran

"The meeting of two personalities is like the contact of two chemical substances: if there is any reaction, both are transformed. What counts in making a happy marriage is not so much how compatible you are, but how you deal with incompatibility." - Anon.

"The more one does and sees and feels, the more one is able to do, and the more genuine may be one's appreciation of fundamental things like home, and love, and understanding companionship." - Robert Baden-Powell

# 7

# Conclusion

In conclusion, you are not alone. That is why there are so many love quotes out there. People have been going through the same things since, as they say, time immemorial. The important element remains one of hope. No matter what you are going through, remember to take the time to refocus, to remember that you are not alone. That person you love is still there somewhere.

In the beginning of this book, I opened by writing a poem. I'm going to close this by just saying, "Thank you." In my journey through life, I have found that through the people I know, and their stories—coupled with my own experiences—I have found a lot of words I wish to share. The world is full of reasons to give up, but it is also full of people so inspiring who embody the essence of love in the truest possible way.

I believe that such love is a reflection of God, or the Creative Force that goes by so many names. Love is truly the most powerful of gifts and blessings, and to have it in your life is the greatest thing anyone can ask for. Love doesn't save the day—that's just in the movies; however, it does make life sweet and give you hope and courage when it seems increasingly hard to find.

The other thing about love is that it requires much maintenance, care, investment, and reinvestment. If you are reading this book and looking at this concluding chapter, I humbly hope you gain the strength and inspiration from the words of people who have been where you are now attempting to traverse in your own living heartship; facing love in all its beauty, power, and complexity. Keep going.

### Final Thoughts and Encouragement

Inspirational love quotes to guide your relationship

After reading through this collection, I hope you have found much enjoyment, with a bit of inspiration and motivation to take some positive action in your life! Relationships are purposeful exercises of growth to do at every moment of the opportunities we are given to interact with those around us. So say yes to embracing the experience; it encourages us to respond, evolve and improve all the time if we let it! Leading into this collection, it can be incredibly difficult or improbable to foresee what we can and will go through within our relationships over time – it can feel quite delicate and daunting to think of how we must rise to face that unknown. Especially fortunately, during all those thousands of times we manage to reach improvement and healthier connection over deteriorating communication, there will be a guide we can listen to.

As a writer, sometimes we are hesitant to like or accept praise because we want to grow and improve our works; it can feel limiting or risky to allow our work to be summarized. But, I want to express my appreciation and all humility that I have had the wonderful opportunity to have you on this ride with me as I continue to share a topic that is very near and dear to my heart. Love is a wonderful phenomenon in our lives, and it is ever-present. Everyone needs a good word or excerpt to remind them of this every now and again, because love, is often though ever-present, is often not at the front-and-center of our experiences. If you ever have some time or need a quick pick-me-up, remember that you can come back here and be reminded all over again.

Milton Keynes UK
Ingram Content Group UK Ltd.
UKHW031450061124
450821UK00004B/495

9 798330 521104